Queen

This book belongs to:

  Macarons

DISCOVER the STORY of

with Beartific

Marie Antoinette

KATELYN LONAS

Table of Contents

Introduction

Marie Antoinette was the last Queen of France, who's known for her expensive taste and love for sweets.

Discover her story marked by controversy, a lavish lifestyle, and the downfall of the French monarchy.

Early Life

Maria Antonia Josepha Johanna was born at the Hofburg Palace in Austria on November 2, 1755.

She was the youngest daughter and 15th child of the Holy Roman Emperor Francis I and Maria Theresa.

Marie Antoinette's Early Life

Francis I

Maria Theresa

Marie Antoinette was born into royalty as a princess of the House of Habsburg and spent her childhood with her older sister, Maria Carolina.

The House of Habsburg was recognized as a prominent German royal family.

The Habsburgs were one of the most influential and wealthy European dynasties, gaining significant power and political influence through royal marriages.

Education

Marie Antoinette's studies were primarily focused on preparing her for her roles and duties as Queen.

Her tutors described her as intelligent but difficult to teach due to her laziness and frivolous behavior.

As a child, Marie Antoinette struggled with basic writing and communication skills.

She was taught German, French, and Italian.

Music greatly enhanced her intellect, as she became skilled in playing the harp, harpsichord, and flute.

Additionally, Antoinette excelled in singing and dancing under the guidance of her music teachers.

Marie Antoinette's Education

Harpsichord

Flute

Harp

7

Marriage

Marie Antoinette was arranged to marry Louis XVI, who was the future King of France.

This marriage was part of a political strategy aimed at strengthening the alliance between Austria and France.

The goal of this marriage was to end conflicts and secure lasting peace between the two nations.

This was significant as it represented a shift toward reconciliation between historically rival powers.

Marie Antoinette and Louis XVI were married on May 16, 1770, at the Royal Chapel in Versailles, France.

At the time of their wedding, Marie Antoinette was 14 years old, and Louis XVI was 15 years old.

Marie Antoinette's wedding dress was crafted from silver cloth and adorned with an array of diamonds.

During their relationship, Marie Antoinette and Louis XVI faced intense public scrutiny and harsh criticism.

A significant challenge they faced was the difficulty in producing an heir to secure the monarchy's future.

It took nearly eight years after their wedding for them to welcome their first child.

Marie Antoinette and Louis XVI had four children:

First Child: Marie Therese Charlotte, born in 1778.

Second Child: Louis Joseph, born in 1781.

Third Child: Louis Charles, born in 1785.

Fourth Child: Sophie Helene Beatrix, born in 1786.

Lifestyle

On May 10, 1774, Marie Antoinette became the Queen of France.

As Queen, she was known for her lavish lifestyle, which included significant spending on portraits and entertainment.

Marie Antoinette had a deep appreciation for the arts and frequently commissioned artists to create works that highlighted her royal image.

Her official portrait painter was Elisabeth Louise Vigee Le Brun, who created around 30 masterpieces of Antoinette in only six years.

Antoinette was very fond of playing cards and billiards.

Her favorite card game was called lansquenet, where she played to win gold pieces.

She spent lots of money on these games, often winning and losing large sums.

Marie Antoinette loved animals, and her residence at the Palace of Versailles was home to many dogs, cats, and monkeys.

Some of her beloved dogs were a pug named Mops, a papillon named Coco, and a spaniel named Thisbe.

Additionally, Antoinette owned a dog kennel made of velvet and silk, which is now part of the Metropolitan Museum of Art's Collection.

Marie Antoinette had a very caring and compassionate nature, as she adopted and fostered numerous children.

After the death of her maid, Antoinette adopted her child, Ernestine, and raised her like her own daughter.

She also took care of Jean Amilcar, who was an enslaved child, and paid for him to receive an education.

Antoinette was commonly known for hosting grand balls, lively performances, and extravagant parties that would last all night.

These events were a significant part of her life at the Palace of Versailles.

Marie Antoinette was also fond of the dramatic arts.

She enjoyed attending performances, such as plays, operas, and ballet shows.

In 1778, the architect Richard Mique constructed Antoinette, a private theatre at the Palace of Versailles.

This theatre had a seating capacity for 250 guests.

Fashion

In the world of fashion, Marie Antoinette became extremely influential, as she popularized various styles and started new trends.

She was most recognized for her elaborate hairstyles and extravagant gowns.

Antoinette popularized the pouf hairstyle, which was known for its dramatic height and decorations.

This hairstyle featured accessories such as ribbons, feathers, and flowers.

She worked with her hairdresser Leonard Autie to achieve this look and inspired many French noblewomen to follow.

During her lifetime, the French court favored muted and darker colors in fashion and decor choices.

However, Marie Antoinette had a preference for brighter and more pastel colors.

She introduced pink and blue to the royal palace, which transformed the color palette of the court.

Marie Antoinette had around 300 custom dresses created every year for her wardrobe.

The majority of these dresses were designed by her couturier, Rose Bertin, who's commonly referred to as the first fashion designer.

These dresses featured pastel-colored silks with ribbons, ruffles, and jewels.

Additionally, Antoinette had an extensive jewelry collection featuring pearls, diamonds, and sapphires.

Among her collection was a diamond and pearl pendant.

This pendant was sold at auction for $36.2 million.

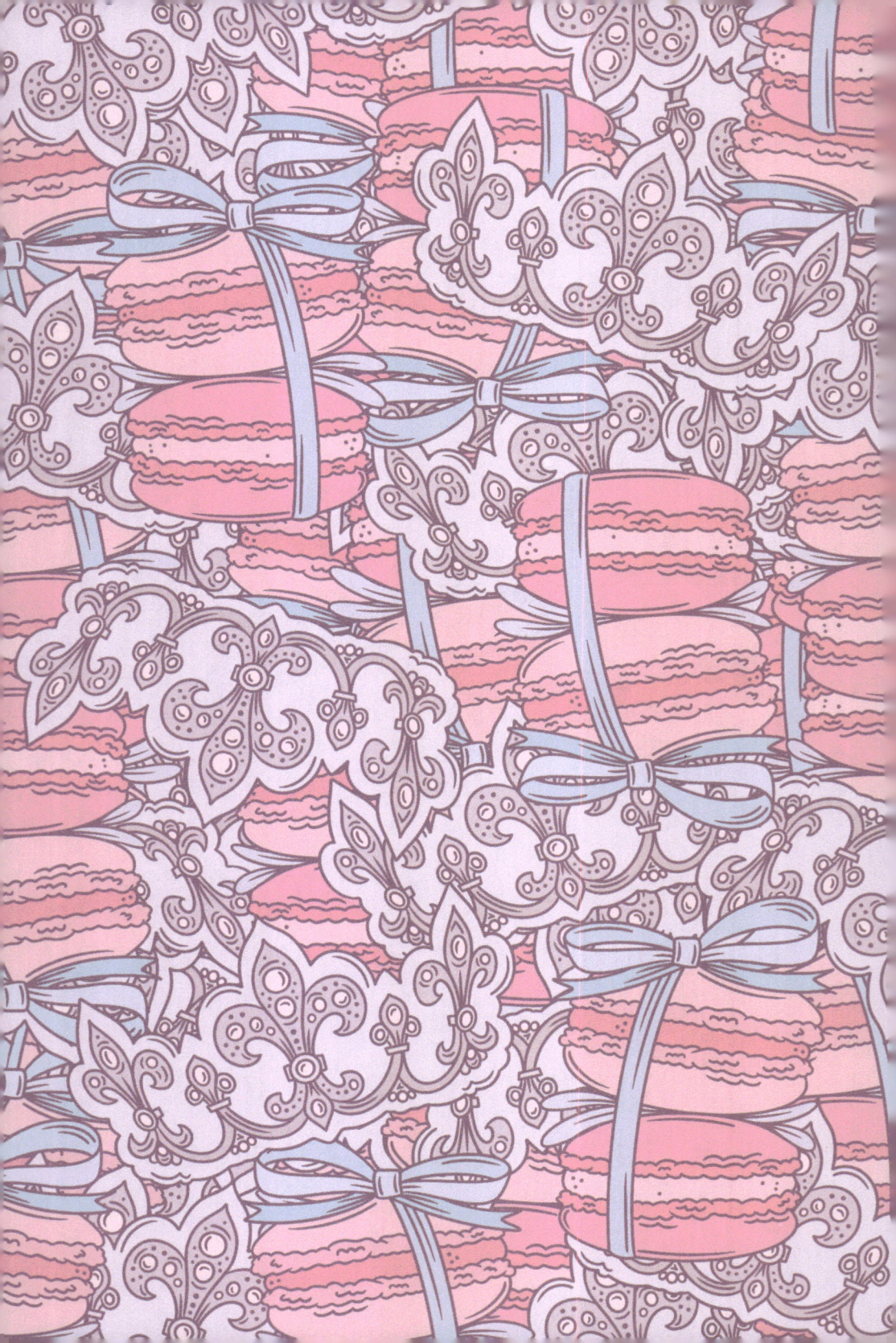

Sweets

One of Marie Antoinette's most well-known traits was her cravings for desserts.

She was renowned for her love of cake, which became a symbol of the luxury and extravagance enjoyed by the French monarchy.

Antoinette was very fond of chocolate and sugar, as her favorite beverages were hot chocolate with whipped cream and orange blossom-flavored sugar water.

Additionally, she had a personal chocolatier who held the title of "Chocolate Maker to the Queen."

Some of the desserts Marie Antoinette enjoyed include traditional macarons, croissants, and petit fours.

Croissant

Petit Fours

27

Diamond

The Affair of the Diamond Necklace was a major scandal that unfolded between 1784 and 1785.

This incident severely tarnished the reputation of Marie Antoinette and the royal family.

It all started in 1772 when two Parisian jewelers, Boehmer and Bassenge, crafted a necklace valued around 1.5 million livres, featuring 647 diamonds, weighing 2,800 carats.

The jewelers intended to sell the diamond necklace to King Louis XV, but he unfortunately passed away before its completion.

Boehmer and Bassenge then presented this necklace to the new rulers, Louis XVI and Marie Antoinette.

However, Antoinette refused to purchase it, stating that she had enough diamonds.

Desperate to sell the necklace, the jewelers were approached by a lady named Comtesse de La Motte, who promised to facilitate the sale of the necklace to Queen Marie Antoinette.

Unknown to everyone, Comtesse de La Motte was a thief and a conwoman.

La Motte successfully manipulated a man named Cardinal de Rohan into believing that she was in the Queen's confidence.

The conwoman convinced the Cardinal that Marie Antoinette secretly desired the necklace and urged him to purchase it on her behalf to regain her favor.

Comtesse de La Motte had promised Cardinal de Rohan that she would deliver the necklace to the Queen.

However, instead of delivering the necklace, she fled and sold all of its diamonds.

This scandal came to light when the jewelers did not receive their payment and discovered that Marie Antoinette was never given the diamond necklace.

Ultimately, the truth was revealed, and all those involved in this scandal were brought to trial.

Unfortunately, the people of France blamed Marie Antoinette for this incident, despite her innocence.

As a result, her reputation was completely damaged and never fully recovered.

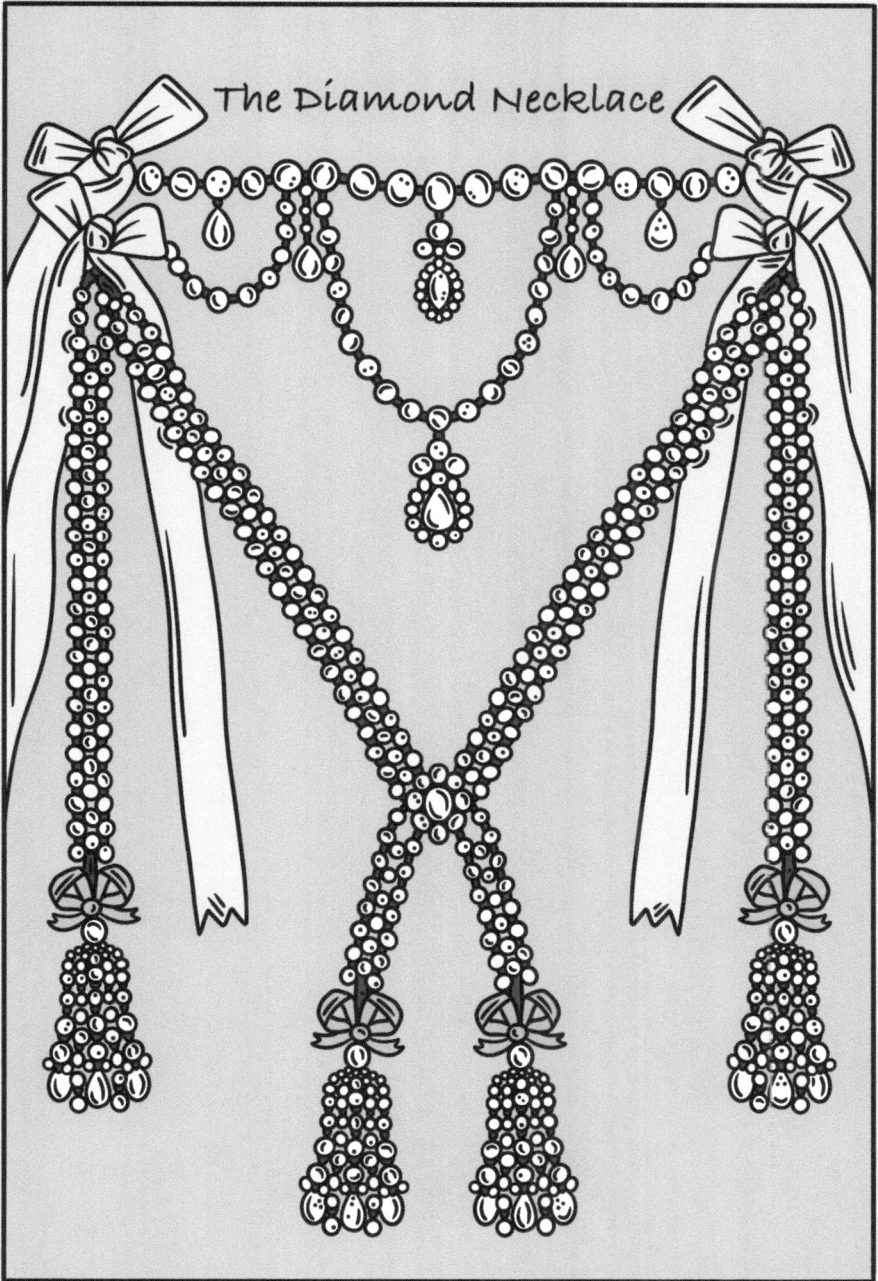

The Diamond Necklace

Public Image

In the beginning of Marie Antoinette's reign as Queen of France, she was loved and adored by many.

Her beauty and youth captivated the public, and they viewed her as a beacon of hope for the monarchy.

As time passed, Antoinette's popularity declined.

Several factors contributed to her negative image:

Her excessive spending on dresses, jewelry, and sweets was criticized, especially when France's economic situation worsened.

As a result, the public began to view her as out of touch with the struggles faced by ordinary citizens.

Additionally, her gambling habits were brought to the public's attention, which created further resentment among the French people as they began to view her as irresponsible and wasteful.

In the end, Antoinette's reputation was destroyed after the diamond necklace scandal, which caused the public to firmly believe she was deceitful and corrupt.

Due to the resentment towards Marie Antoinette and the French monarchy, numerous rumors began to circulate among the public.

⸱⸱⟩⟫ ⟪⟪ ⟨⸱⸱

One of the most infamous rumors attributed to Marie Antoinette was the phrase "Let them eat cake."

Supposedly this phrase was Marie Antoinette's response to the suffering of the poor who could not afford bread.

However, there is no credible evidence that she actually said this.

This quote is viewed as revolutionary propaganda aimed at depicting Marie Antoinette as out of touch with the people during a time of economic crisis.

Ultimately, this negative perception contributed to her downfall, as Marie Antoinette became the last Queen of France.

Revolution

The French Revolution began on July 14, 1789, and ended on November 9, 1799.

This revolution arose due to the poor standard of living of the common people and the increasing unpopularity of the French monarchy.

In the beginning of the Revolution, Louis XVI was hesitant to leave France.

He was determined to uphold the monarchy, and Marie Antoinette did not want to abandon him during this crisis.

However, as the Revolution progressed and conditions became more dangerous, Louis XVI and Marie Antoinette decided to flee with their children.

On the night of June 20, 1791, Marie Antoinette and her family attempted to escape from Paris.

To evade detection, the royal family disguised themselves as servants and traveled in carriages.

The royal family intended to reach Montmedy, which was a fortress located near the eastern border of France.

During this time, Montmedy was home to a large force of troops that remained loyal to the French monarchy.

The royal family believed this fortress would serve as a safe haven where they could find protection.

Marie Antoinette and Louis XVI hoped to gather support from the loyalist troops stationed in Montmedy to initiate a counter-revolution.

Their ultimate goal was to regain power and restore their authority.

However, on this journey, Louis XVI was recognized in Sainte-Menehould by a postmaster, who identified him from a portrait that had been widely circulated.

The royal family was arrested in Varennes and brought back to Paris.

This failed escape attempt became known as the Flight to Varennes and resulted in significant consequences for the royal family.

Following this incident, more of the radicals pushed for the abolition of the monarchy and demanded that the royal family be put on trial for treason.

In August 1792, several thousand revolutionaries stormed the Tuileries Palace, which was the residence of the royal family.

Marie Antoinette and her family were then imprisoned at the Temple and remained there to await trial.

The end of royal rule occurred on September 21, 1792, as the monarchy was officially abolished by the National Convention.

Execution

On January 21, 1793, Louis XVI was found guilty of high treason and beheaded.

After his execution, Marie Antoinette was separated from her children and got transferred to a new prison called the Conciergerie.

Marie Antoinette was tried on October 14, 1793, by the Revolutionary Tribunal, which was a court instituted by the National Convention.

Antoinette faced serious charges of treason and immoral behavior with her children and others.

During her trial, Marie Antoinette's son, Louis Charles, was manipulated into testifying against her.

Despite these intense circumstances, Antoinette was described as remaining brave and calm throughout the proceedings.

Her trial lasted for two days, concluding with her being found guilty of treason and sentenced to death by guillotine.

Before her execution, Marie Antoinette's final words were, "Pardon me, sir, I did not do it on purpose."

She said this statement after accidentally stepping on the foot of her executioner, Charles-Henri Sanson.

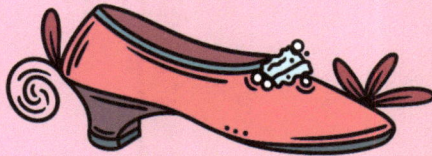

At the age of 37, Marie Antoinette was beheaded at the Place de la Concorde on October 16, 1793.

After her execution, they dumped her body in an unmarked grave.

However, in 1815 Marie Antoinette's remains were moved and given a proper burial in France at the Basilica of Saint-Denis.

In the end, Antoinette's only surviving child was Marie Therese Charlotte, who made it into adulthood after the French Revolution.

Legacy

Today, Marie Antoinette plays a significant role in various aspects of life.

She continues to inspire designers around the world, and her story is frequently told and referenced in films, literature, and music.

Marie Antoinette is a very controversial and complex historical figure who made major impacts on society.

As Antoinette's life and tragic fate have inspired numerous works.

Some individuals portray Marie Antoinette as a villain, often highlighting her excessive spending and blaming her for the downfall of the French monarchy.

On the other hand, people also sympathize with Marie Antoinette as they see her as a young girl who was not prepared for the pressures and responsibilities that come with becoming Queen.

Marie Antoinette's story continues to spark debates and discussions regarding her historical role.

Nevertheless, it's undeniable that she left a tremendous imprint on the fashion world.

The Last Queen of France
- Marie Antoinette -

The End!

remember to:

BELIEVE
DREAM
ACHIEVE

Author & Illustrator

Katelyn Lonas

Katelyn is an 18-year-old from Southern California who has a passion for inspiring others to believe in themselves and chase after their dreams! At the age of 9, she wrote and illustrated her first book and since then went on to publish 75 more books! Katelyn hopes you enjoyed reading about Marie Antoinette and are excited for more stories to come!

-Katelyn Lonas

www.ingramcontent.com/pod-product-compliance
Lightning Source LLC
Chambersburg PA
CBHW041522090426

42737CB00037B/12